My Country
South Africa

Cath Senker

D0452692

FRANKLIN WATTS

This edition copyright ©
Franklin Watts 2014

Franklin Watts
338 Euston Road
London NW1 3BH

Franklin Watts Australia
Level 17/207 Kent Street
Sydney, NSW 2000

All rights reserved.

Dewey number: 968'.068
ISBN: 978 1 4451 2704 0

Printed in Malaysia

Series Editor: Paul Rockett
Series Designer: Paul Cherrill for
  Basement68
Picture Researcher: Diana Morris

Franklin Watts is a division of
Hachette Children's Books,
an Hachette UK company.

www.hachette.co.uk

Every attempt has been made to clear copyright. Should there
be any inadvertent omission please apply to the publisher for
rectification.

Picture credits: auremar/Shutterstock: 13t; Marta Benavides/
istockphoto: front cover cl; Kevin Calvin/Alamy: 12; Alexander
Chaikin/Shutterstock: 7t; Tor Eigeland/Alamy: front cover c, 4,
13b, 16b, 22; Fretschi/Shutterstock: 20b; Robert Fried/Alamy:
15; Botond Horvath/Shutterstock: 9; Pierre Jacques/Hemis/
Alamy: 11; JeniFoto/Shutterstock: 5; Robert Linton/istockphoto:
13c; Maugli/Shutterstock: 1, 21; Phillip Minnis /Shutterstock: 20t;
mountainpix /Shutterstock: 3, 17t; Luba V Nel/Shutterstock:
19; PHB.cz Richard Semik/Shutterstock: 7b; Photononstop/
Superstock: 10; Radius/Superstock: 14; Ray Roberts/Alamy:
16c; Samot/Shutterstock: 2, 8; Paul Tavener/Alamy: 18; Paul
Villecourt/Watts: 6; witchcraft/Shutterstock: front cover cr;
Stephan Zabel/istockphoto: 17b.

 Contents

All words in **bold** appear in the glossary on page 23.

South Africa in the world

Howzit! My name is Mandisa and I come from South Africa.

Pretoria
Johannesburg
Drakensberg Mountains
Khayelitsha

South Africa's place in the world.

South Africa is a medium-sized country at the southern tip of the continent of Africa.

I live in Khayelitsha
(say 'ky-ul-it-sha'), a large
township — a place where
mostly black Africans live.
It is crowded and noisy,
but it's home!

children playing
in the streets
of Khayelitsha
in winter.

People who live in South Africa

Black, white and Asian people live in the main cities.

Around 49 million people live in South Africa. Most are black Africans.

There are also Asians and white people, and people from other African countries.

About two-thirds of South Africans live in cities. The biggest cities are Johannesburg, Cape Town, Durban and Pretoria. Pretoria is the **capital**.

The rest live in the countryside and work in farming. They tend to be poorer than the people in the cities.

Zulu children in the countryside – the girl wears a traditional costume.

What South Africa looks like

South Africa has different **landscapes**. In the centre is a high plateau — a large, flat area. In the north is the baking hot Kalahari **Desert**.

The red sands of the Kalahari Desert.

Around the plateau are hills and mountains. The highest are the Drakensberg Mountains to the east.

The country has a long **coastline** with beaches. The eastern coastline has plenty of rain. The land there is lush and green.

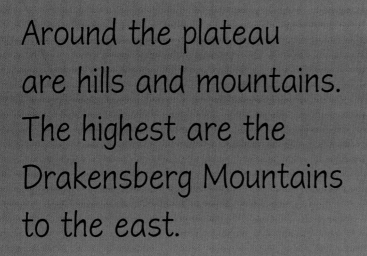

The mountains are covered in snow in winter - perfect for skiing and trekking.

At home with my family

My dad is reading a story to my little brother in our living room.

Many people in Khayelitsha and other townships live in **shacks** made from wood and tin.

We have a TV, but most people in townships just listen to the radio.

Some parts of Khayelitsha do not have electricity or **running water** in their homes.

We children have to help out at home. I help to look after my little brother and sister.

children often go to fetch water from an outdoor pump.

What we eat

Mum cooks rice on a small stove.

My favourite food is chicken — it's our special treat once a week.

We mostly eat cheap foods such as rice and beans. We use a lot of **maize** in our cooking.

Better-off people in South Africa often eat meat. Barbecues are popular. They are called *braai*.

South Africans also eat foods from different countries, such as Indian curries.

A family enjoys a delicious outdoor barbecue with vegetables.

13

Going to school

South African children start school when they are five or six. When they are 12, they start secondary school. Most parents have to pay for their children to go to school. In the poorest places, there are free schools.

My class at school.

 # Having fun

The family is important to all South Africans. We like to spend our free time with close family and our aunts, uncles, grandparents and cousins. I have lots of cousins!

In the townships, people often play football in the street.

In South Africa, our favourite sport is football. I play nearly every day.

We make our own toys and games. I like rolling old car tyres in the street.

My cousin rolls a tyre to see how far it will go!

Festivals and celebrations

Lively christian worship in the province of KwaZulu-Natal.

For us, Christmas is a summer holiday.

Most South Africans are Christians, so Christmas and Easter are important events.

There are also Muslims, Hindus, Jews and people who follow African religions. They celebrate their own **festivals**.

We have several festivals to remember important dates in South African history. Freedom Day is on 27 April, when we celebrate our first **democratic election** held in 1994.

A joyful celebration of Freedom Day.

Things to see

South Africa has some amazing sights. Around Cape Town, you can learn about big birds and visit beautiful beaches. South Africa has dense forests too.

If you visit Boulders Beach, near Cape Town, you'll see penguins!

At a national park, you can go on a **safari** to see wildlife. You'll spot lions, leopards, elephants and rhinos.

In the townships you can find out about the **local** African **culture** and listen to African music.

An elephant lumbers across the road in Kruger National Park.

Here are some facts about my country!

Fast facts about South Africa

Capital city = South Africa has three capital cities: Pretoria, Cape Town and Bloemfontein.

Population = 49 million

Currency = the Rand

Area = 1,219,090km²

Languages = 11 main languages. These ones are spoken by the most people: Afrikaans, English, IsiZulu, Sepedi

National holiday = Christmas Day

Main religions = Christian, Muslim, Hindu and African religions

Longest river = Orange River (2,200km)

Highest mountain = Mafadi (3,450m)

Glossary

capital the most important city in a country

coastline the land along a coast

culture the language, food, music and way of life of a group of people

democratic election when all adults in a country can vote to decide who will rule them

desert a hot, dry area with little rain

festival a special time when people celebrate something

landscape what a place looks like

local to do with the place where you live

maize also known as sweetcorn, with grains that are made into flour

running water water that enters buildings in pipes and comes out of taps

safari a trip to see wild animals

shack a small building, usually made from wood or metal

township a town on the edge of a South African city

Websites

www.factmonster.com/ipka/A0934644.html
Basic facts about the country.

http://kids.nationalgeographic.com/kids/places/find/south-africa
Facts, photos and maps.

Books

Been There! South Africa by Annabel Savery (Franklin Watts, 2011)

Countries in Our World: South Africa by Alison Brownlie Bojang (Franklin Watts, 2012)

Index